THE REWARD: STRATEGICALLY ALIGNED

INCENTIVE PLANNING

ASHRAF ELTOMI

Join our blog to learn how to motivate and manage change in your business at:

www.bespokepublishinghouse.com

WHY I WROTE THIS BOOK

Every company has a top employee, its shining star. The one you can count on to close the sale or get things done. Imagine if all employees were top performers working to their full potential. Creating such an environment is a tough challenge, it encompasses building a continuous development environment, keeping employees satisfied, challenged and motivated. Humans needs and behaviors vary, but with the right formula (incentive plan) you can trigger each individual to unleash the beast within. The key to motivation is creating a collaborative competitive environment and establishing multiple complimentary targets. And of course acknowledging accomplishments with the proper uncapped, competitor relative reward according to employees' needs.

Your employees are your most valuable assets. Take care of them and keep them motivated and they will take care of your business and clientele. Without the proper incentive plan companies will struggle to reach their goals. Top management must optimize formal appraisals and financial reward systems to encourage the front line officers in reinforcing efforts to achieve corporate goals. The incentive compensation policy must be in line with corporate strategy and goals. There are several elements of an incentive plan: financial instruments, performance measures, degree of discretion in allocating rewards, size and frequency of rewards, degree of uniformity and funding. These elements must be tailored according to the product/service life cycle, market dynamics, interdivisional and corporate relationships.

I have seen successful teams all over the world fall a part due to inadequate bonus structures. In some cases it has been detrimental for their businesses. Often administration puts together an inherited incentive system without any consideration of business dynamics and the company's life cycle. This book is an attempt to offer the proper tools and mentality to reach an efficient and motivational incentive plan for any business.

WHY YOU SHOULD READ THIS BOOK

This is a comprehensive top notch book on incentive planning that will help each reader learn the art of People Management based on an eclectic approach that uses multiple personality theories with the aim of bringing harmony to the workplace; dealing with employees as human beings, where job satisfaction and corporate goals go together hand in hand, in a realistic and efficient approach.

A must read for CEOs, Executives, Team Leaders, Sales Managers, HR Managers or anyone wanting to learn about incentives.

How to motivate cost effectively? What to evaluate; corporate vs personal goals? Formula-based incentive structure or not? Uncapped? How frequent? How to fund? Are some questions that are answered in this book with a practical solution for your business.

TABLE OF CONTENTS

Why I Wrote this Book

Why You Should Read This Book

Chapter 1. Collaborative Competition

Chapter 2. Strategy Driven Compensation Structure

Chapter 3. Motivation and Incentive

Chapter 4. Performance Measures

Chapter 5. Degree of Discretion

Chapter 6. Size and Frequency

Chapter 7. Funding Method

Chapter 8. Change Management

Exhibit 1

Exhibit 2

Refererences

About the Author

CHAPTER 1. COLLABORATIVE COMPETITION

Competition in the workplace can be either positive or negative according to how employees emotionally interpret it. Top organizations are starting to adopt a distinctly collaborative approach to achieve success and build high-performing teams. Negative competition is a short-term strategy with long-term consequences. Positive competition aims to further team sustainability and organizational longevity.

Here are 3 ways to leverage competition to drive workplace collaboration:

1. Find out what motivates your individual team members and capitalize on those intrinsic/extrinsic motivators.

You need to first determine what intrinsic/extrinsic motivators most strongly affect each team member. This will better enable you to predict what forms of competition are most effective.

For example, someone who is just starting in a new position might be more inclined to want to prove themselves to the group and develop their own self-worth (an intrinsic motivator) as opposed to someone who has been working at the same company for a few years and is more concerned about how much they're currently being paid commensurate to their experience (an extrinsic motivator). As a side note, be sure to always keep those motivators positive!

2. Focus on the team, not on individuals.

As with any competition, there are winners and losers. Make your team members feel like they belong to an Olympic sports team, where even coming in dead last still places them among the best of the best. And when it comes to ranking each team member's performance, it's easy to give all the credit to just the top contributors and to overlook everyone else's efforts.

It's true, while recognizing an employee's exceptional performance is undoubtedly important, try to recognize each team member's individual achievements as well. Avoid playing favorites and in giving preferential treatment to only the top contributors. Always keep in mind that the primary reason for establishing workplace collaborative competition is to reach some sort of common goal as a team, so keep it positive by focusing on what the team has already accomplished together, not only on what needs to be done.

3. Make competition about group learning and sharing.

Don't be an idea-hoarder. When working together, it's critical to make sure each team member shares their knowledge with the group. Doing so not only presents a valuable learning opportunity for each team member, but it can also help advance your organization's goals. Additionally, sharing your ideas with the group can be a great way to receive feedback, allowing you to further re-examine your own ideas. In short, don't withhold information at the expense of your team.

MULTIPLE COMPLIMENTARY TARGETS

It's very common for managers to game the metrics to their advantage, accelerating revenue or postponing expenditures are a few obvious examples. Rather than focusing on the short term, an incentive plan with multiple targets will deliver real sustainable value for the business.

Studies have shown that executives who had to achieve multiple goals to receive their bonuses were just as likely to miss a given target as they were to exceed it. Statistically, this is what you'd expect to see if no manipulation has taken place. In contrast, it is highly unlikely statistically that executives will just overperform most of the time. Such results are an indication that they are actively managing to their targets.

When you set multiple targets, make sure they aren't too closely correlated to prevent any crossover. There is no magic number of targets to choose. Ultimately, it comes down to which metrics reflect the corporation's strategic objectives. A good rule of thumb, however, is to aim for three to five, because using just two could still create opportunities to manage to the targets while more than five can create confusion about where the organization should focus.

Employees are motivated by two goals, either a sense of achievement or a pay check. Offering an additional reward motivates employees to go above and beyond and creates a pleasant and healthy work environment. Employees must know that hard word pays of well, both financially and with recognition of achievement. In turn productivity increases and hence the bottom line increases much higher than the monetary rewards distributed.

Creating such an environment demonstrates mutual respect between management and amongst staff and will help retain top talent. This helps unite the team and creates an open channel for communication. Effectively, with the right incentive, employees will personalize corporate goals and will speak one language, reflecting your values and will be brand ambassadors in the market.

It's imperative to respect employees' needs in tailoring the incentive plan, weighing in the financial reward whilst maintaining a healthy work life balance.

CHAPTER 2. STRATEGY DRIVEN COMPENSATION STRUCTURE

The first step in designing an incentive compensation plan is to establish company strategy in relevance to three main areas of concern:

PRODUCT/SERVICE LIFE CYCLE – profit trade-offs expected according to the product's progress stage from introduction to growth, maturity and decline

MARKET DYNAMICS – industry external factors affecting your business model. Different performance rewards are tailored according to the specific stage of the industry. Companies operating in innovative markets will adopt and enhance an entrepreneurial approach in establishing new markets and products. Whilst companies in mature industries focus on market share and customer relationship management. The incentive plan will have to factor these different approaches.

INTERDIVISIONAL AND CORPORATE RELATIONSHIP – According to how different divisions in a company collaborate or operate independently, the incentive plan will be different in each case. If corporate management is involved advising managers directly, the incentive plan should not be the same if they are operating autonomously.

FINANCIAL INSTRUMENTS

HOW TO MOTIVATE COST EFFECTIVELY

Most employees prefer cash bonus systems as incentives. However, it's considered best practice to also utilize another form of incentive to supplement cash payments to maximize motivation of behavior. This can be in the form of current stock, deferred cash and phantom options. Any mix of alternatives can be made keeping in mind stages of product life cycle and market dynamics.

Stock awards tend to adhere personal interest with the long term interest of the corporation. However, on the long term, stock awards can have a negative financial consequence on corporate and stockholders. Therefore, stock options should be limited to top management and presidents.

Chapter 3. Motivation and Incentive

What forces are behind our actions? Do you get up and head to the gym each day because you know its good for you, or is it because of some type of external reward? There are many different reasons why we do things. Sometimes we are motivated to act because of internal desires and wishes, but at other times, our behaviors are driven by a desire for external rewards.

According to one theory of human motivation, our actions are often inspired by a desire to gain outside reinforcement. The incentive theory is one of the major theories of motivation and suggests that behavior is motivated by a desire for reinforcement or incentives.

Development of Incentive Theory to Explain Human Behavior

Incentive theory began to emerge during the 1940s and 1950s, building on the earlier drive theories established by psychologists such as Clark Hull.

How exactly does this theory account for human behaviors? Rather than focus on more intrinsic forces behind motivation, the incentive theory proposes that people are pulled toward behaviors that lead to rewards and pushed away from actions that might lead to negative consequences.

Two people may act in different ways in the same situation based entirely on the types of incentives that are available to them at that time.

You can probably think of many different situations where your behavior was directly influenced by the promise of a reward or punishment. Perhaps you studied for an exam in order to get a good grade, ran a marathon in order to receive recognition, or took a new position at work in order to get a raise. All of these actions were influenced by an incentive to gain something in return for your efforts.

How Does Incentive Theory Work?

In contrast with other theories that suggest we are pushed into action by internal drives (such as the drive-reduction theory of motivation, arousal theory, and instinct theory), incentive theory instead suggests that we are pulled into action by outside incentives.

You can liken incentive theory to operant conditioning. Just as in operant conditioning, where behaviors are performed in order to either gain reinforcement or avoid punishment, incentive theory states that your actions are directed toward gaining rewards.

What type of rewards? Think about what type of things motivate you to study hard and do well in school. Good grades are one type of incentive. Gaining esteem and accolades from your teachers and parents might be another. Money is also an excellent example of an external reward that motivates behavior. In many cases, these external rewards can motivate you to do things that you might otherwise avoid such as chores, work, and other tasks you might find unpleasant.

OBSERVATIONS ABOUT INCENTIVE THEORY:

Incentives can be used to get people to engage in certain behaviors, but they can also be used to get people to stop performing certain actions.

Incentives only become powerful if the individual places importance on the reward.

Rewards have to be obtainable in order to be motivating. For example, a student will not be motivated to earn a top grade on an exam if the assignment is so difficult that it is not realistically achievable.

WHY SOME INCENTIVES ARE MORE MOTIVATING THAN OTHERS

Obviously, not all incentives are created equal and the rewards that you find motivating might not be enough to inspire another person to take action. Physiological, social, and cognitive factors can all play a role in what incentives you find motivating.

For example, you are more likely to be motivated by food when you are actually hungry versus when you are full. A teenage boy might be motivated to clean his room by the promise of a coveted video game while another person would find such a game completely unappealing.

"The value of an incentive can change over time and in different situations," notes author Stephen L. Franzoi in his text Psychology: A Discovery Experience. "For example, gaining praise from your parents may have positive incentive value for you in some situations, but not in others. When you are home, your parents' praise may be a positive incentive. However, when your friends visit, you may go out of your way to avoid receiving parental praise, because your friends may tease you."

COMPENSATION MIX

"Incentive" does not necessarily equal "cash." Rewards come in many forms, and what's motivating to one team or individual isn't necessarily what would entice another. A big part of getting your incentive plan right is knowing what form of compensation will be most effective.

Take a look at these data from the CBPR:

HOW ORGANIZATIONS REWARD/RECOGNIZE HIGH-PERFORMING EMPLOYEES

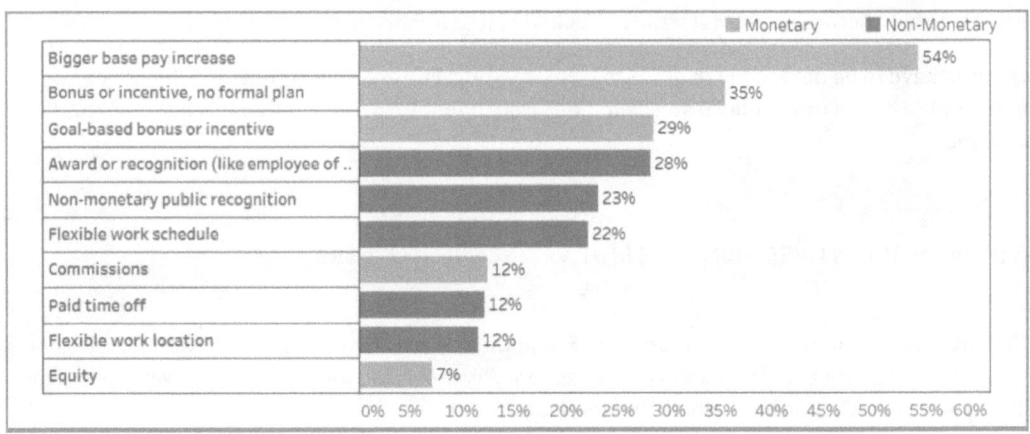

As the report says, "Responses within the 'other' category ranged from verbal expressions of gratitude, to vacations and trips, to preference for plumb project assignments. Learning and development also featured prominently in the 'other' category.

"Top-performing companies are more likely to reward high-performing employees with monetary rewards. They exceeded typical companies in all monetary rewards, especially goal-based bonuses (35 percent vs. 28 percent) and bigger base pay increases (58 percent vs. 54 percent)."

Think about what makes sense for your organization before jumping straight to "give them money."

Chapter 4. Performance Measures

Corporate vs Personal Goals

Ideally, a mix of both would be best, or an additional indicator could be applied. Some examples include, sales, profit as percentage of sales, return on assets and achievement of management objectives. In adopting this mix methodology it's crucial to emphasize the commitment of the welfare of the whole company, stressing on interdivisional cooperation and minimize any divisional self interest. Unrelated business units' incentive plan should obviously factor in on a single measure of its own profitability, but still incorporating a minimal factor for corporate goals would be beneficial. This will be featured in our incentive plan model further in Exhibit 2.

Please note that performance measures used also affect the product life cycle problem.

Relative Targets

Targets can be very powerful but if they are established without proper consideration of the global changes underway today they can be meaningless or lead an organization towards failure. Targets must be based on the future; they must define a change towards a defined and desirable future situation. Organizations need to establish a good understanding of the future operating environment in order to set meaningful targets – the future will not resemble the recent past. Targets need to be a part of a coherent future-focused strategy.

Most compensation packages set absolute goals, meaning that the CEO must hit a specific number to receive a bonus. In fact, the use of absolute goals has become increasingly pervasive over the past decade. In 2006 the payouts of 82% of CEOs and 89% of all top executives were pegged to them; by 2014 those numbers had risen to 93% and 98%, respectively.

It's certainly an easy approach. The board can just use analysts' forecasts to determine a goal, and the CEO gets a clear number to measure progress against. If you're feeling bold, the next time you're in a senior executive's office, ask whether his or her computer has a ticker active on it that tracks the company's stock price.

But absolute goals don't necessarily lead firms to reward performance. Say the board decides the appropriate target is 2% revenue growth. With an absolute metric, it would reward a CEO who grew revenue 2% while the sector overall grew 7%, but not a CEO who grew revenue 1.5% while the sector shrank 3%—even though the latter CEO did a better job.

By switching to relative targets, boards can avoid that kind of problem completely. Relative targets also make gaming far harder because the performance of competitors isn't known until they release results, which often happens weeks or months after the end of the performance period. Senior executives can't go back and manipulate numbers at that point. The best way to beat the competition, then, is to continually strive to improve the corporation's performance. The research confirms this: When CEOs had relative targets, company performance was either slightly greater than or slightly less than the relative target with equal likelihood, which is what you would expect in the absence of gaming.

Absolute targets let managers stay in their comfort zones, focusing on things they can more easily control, like R&D spending, SG&A spending, or landing a large contract. They have no incentive to look beyond that. Relative metrics, by contrast, encourage an outward focus: To outdo competitors, executives must also study them closely and find ways to create differentiated positions. Although there's a risk that the focus on rivals will cause some companies to rely too much on benchmarking, this will be balanced by the fact that at least one of them will always be innovating. And if the CEO wants to hit the relative targets in her contract, she can't merely copy those innovations—she'll have to create a distinctive advantage.

In setting relative targets, you need to think carefully about which competitors to follow. This comparison group should also be based on the firm's strategy. If the company is a major player in a mature industry, it will want to use its large competitors as the primary benchmarks. If the corporation is expanding into a new area as the core of its strategy, it should benchmark against smaller, newer rivals in that sector. The sweet spot will be more than one or two (which makes it too easy for the CEO to benchmark against others) and fewer than 10 (since the competitors' performance will have to be aggregated into one number for comparison).

Of course, the exact number of benchmarked competitors will depend on how many publicly owned companies are in the industry, and it's OK to pick bigger or smaller companies, provided you adjust the relevant benchmarks to account for differences with your corporation. For example, if you're a small player going up against a large conglomerate, you can use the results in the specific areas in which you compete with it as your benchmarks (if its results are broken out that granularly) or estimate what portion of its overall performance is accounted for by the division you compete with.

NON FINANCIAL TARGETS

We are used to seeing executives and sales representatives annually rewarded for meeting their direct sales or profit goals. They are often rewarded with an incentive or bonus determined by performance versus management or ownership's expectations. While these direct incentives and rewards are obvious there are also an entire series of incentives that can be also employed to these executives and employees that are based upon less direct measures of performance.

These components (in terms of goals or metrics) are often used with and as a complement to direct sales or profit incentives in order to let the company also focus upon (and pay for) the "building blocks" of sales and profit success in this and future years.

What are examples of these types of indirect goals or metrics? Sales success building blocks include:

Focusing sales force time and attention on those customers with the highest potential;

Convincing current customers to buy and use more of your most profitable and important products;

Assuring that the company's share of market is constantly growing or in line with strategic objectives;

Closing ratios for deals (e.g.: 50% of proposals written); and

Getting the highest price possible on each and every transaction (e.g.: gross profit of the revenue stream).

Similarly, executive (or business-unit) success building blocks include—

Getting your sales force to get the highest price possible on each and every transaction (e.g.: gross profit of revenue stream);

Productivity of capital employed;

Aggressive product development and introduction (keep the product pipeline full);

Control of overhead and cost;

Improving productivity in all aspects of business operations; and

Managing exposure to product, process and people risk and obsolescence.

While you are regularly paying executives for sales and profit success, you are generally also asking them to do the above tasks every day—so why not include some of them in the annual incentive plan, if you do not already do so?

This suggests that a company should rewards its leaders and operators both for those things that happen and can be measured this year (financial quantity and quality), and those things that are building the foundation for this and next year's success (sustainability).

One way to do this is with a mix of pure financial (direct) along with indirect goals and metrics in the annual incentive plan. This trend in incentive design has increasingly gained traction over the last decade. The following are real examples of two such plans:

"The use of these types of indirect incentives can be controversial."

In the sales force—The sales representative is paid an incentive of $0 to $60,000 per year for the growth of their book of accounts versus management's pre-established expectations for success. If the annual goal is achieved, $30,000 is earned. In addition, the sales representative can earn another $0 to $40,000 in the year if they—

Sell over $500,000 of the company's newest and most-profitable product to the sales rep's top 6 volume accounts.

Increase the gross margin of their account portfolio by 2% (nominally), or increase total account profit contribution by $200,000, or more.

In the executive suite—The top divisional executive is paid an annual bonus of $0 to $90,000 based upon the pre-tax profit of the business unit. An amount of $45,000 is earned if $1,000,000 in pre-tax profit is achieved. 2% of pre-tax profit is added to the executive's bonus for all pre-tax profit over $2,000,000. In addition, the executive can earn another $0 to $60,000 in the year if they—

Reduce company general and administrative overhead from 15% of sales to 12% of sales by year's end.

Complete implementation of a new direct sales channel that accounts for (as a running rate) of no less than 10% of company volume by year end.

Introduce a new specific technologically-based product by mid-year and achieve $1,000,000 in sales orders by year's end through all sales channels.

These incentives are sometimes called "non-financial." We prefer to use the term "indirect," because the metrics are generally both financially-based and readily measurable by normal accounting practices and systems. You are simply measuring sales and profit success in a different and more elemental way.

The use of these types of indirect incentives can be controversial. Three basic objections are most often heard.

"These are really discretionary bonuses." Clearly, the examples above are all designed to be quite objective and clear in terms of expectations and reward. Further, simple pay and performance tables can be developed for clarity of communication and ultimate year-end bonus calculation. However, we have seen indirect incentives that do fit the description discretionary. In our world, more objective and measurable metrics are better for everybody.

"They are just too complicated." Well, guilty on that charge! They are clearly more complicated than calculating a percent of sales or percent of pre-tax profit each month. But, your business is surely also much more complicated than the above-stated calculations. In my experience, we have found that we can describe an indirect executive or sales incentive plan on a single (and one-sided) page with accompanying payout rules. I generally also throw in a second page with an example or two, as needed. It just isn't that complicated once you take the plunge.

"Management and ownership will need to spend all of their time on plan administration." It's true only if they like doing plan administration—and some do. The payout tables and rules I described above (combined with a little common sense) make incentive plan administration no more time consuming than a traditional commission plan, and likely less time consuming in the end.

So how do you put these ideas into action for 2020? Try this.

Consider both your sales force and your key executives. Choose three annual goals or metrics for each, (other than enterprise, unit or portfolio sales or profit) for 2020. A hint—start by focusing on improving margin, product mix, quality, or productivity. Tell the sales rep or executive where you will be looking this year and explain your expectations. Then measure and talk about your expectations every month. In our experience, you do not even need to attach money to get results and their attention.

Then, select the same or new indirect goals or metrics for 2021 and do it all over again. But now, make it part of their existing bonus plan, with dollars attached.

Remember, in the end, you are building annual incentives to focus your operators on three imperatives—quantity, quality and sustainability. If you ignore any one of the three you will eventually get into trouble.

Chapter 5. Degree of Discretion

Formula based incentive structure or not

This is directly related to allocated performance measures and the product life cycle. In the same manner, formula based incentive plans must include a factor for corporate goals to enhance their achievement with respect to interdivisional relationships. Quarterly, semi and annual bonuses emphasize the short term, which leads to managers trying to look good by the deadline. Top management should evaluate qualitatively the long run implications of employees' action and tailor the reward system in part on that basis. Further, they need to factor any spikes in their specific industry in the related time horizon for the incentive to be realistic.

Top management, involved directly in the decision making across multiple business units, should enjoy a largely discretionary incentive. This is mainly to retain their influence over business units' strategy and procedures. Further, to factor the less quantifiable aspects of their duties and responsibilities.

CHAPTER 6. SIZE AND FREQUENCY

UNCAPPED? HOW OFTEN?

Incentive rewards must be meaningful and adequate with risks involved. Top management has to study the company's requirements for risk adversity and innovation. When these requirements exceed competitors, higher rewards should be granted for successful executives. Whenever possible, bonuses should be uncapped to motivate employees exponentially.

Depending on the business sales cycle, the frequency of rewards is allocated. Each industry is different, as it influences the time frame of managers and has financial implications that need to be considered.

Incentive Payout Curve

WHAT ARE STEPPED INCENTIVE PAYOUT CURVES?

An incentive payout curve defines the relationship between various levels of performance (the independent variable on the x-axis) and the associated payout amount (the dependent variable on the y-axis) for different levels of performance. A traditional incentive payout curve delivers different payout amounts for performance at various points between a minimum (or "threshold") level of performance and a maximum ("superior" or "stretch") level of performance. Usually, a "target" level of performance is defined to pay out 100% of an employee's target incentive opportunity.

Figure 1 below illustrates a typical incentive plan payout curve. Achievement of the threshold level of performance will immediately generate an incentive payout equal to 50% of target with the payout increasing linearly to 100% of incentive target for the achievement of target performance. The payout then increases linearly between target and superior performance goals, usually with a maximum payout capped at 150% or 200% of target. Among the S&P 100, 38% of the measures used in long-term incentives paid 50% of target for achievement of the threshold goal, while another 34% had some other higher or lower payout step. Only 29% of measures included no step (i.e., payout beginning at zero).

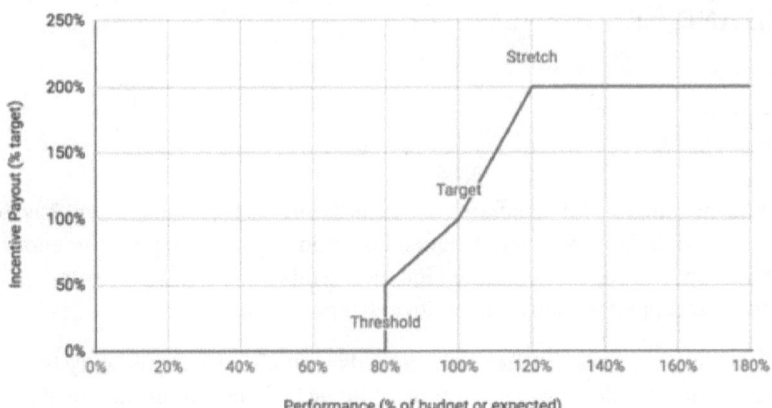

Figure 1. Typical Incentive Payout Curve

As is clear from the illustration, if performance falls short – even by one dollar — of the threshold goal (or whatever unit of performance is measured: one customer, one percentage point, or one widget), then a zero payout is earned. As the incremental dollar, customer or widget is added to results, the calculated payout immediately jumps to 50% of target. Such a stepped payout relationship increases business risk, as described in greater detail below.

History and context: the benefit of a payout step

Traditional payout curves like the one illustrated in Figure 1 have existed for as long as incentive plans have been around. In the early 1990s, the initial step at threshold was heavily influenced by the fact that Earnings Per Share (EPS) was a key and very common measure (and sometimes the only measure) in many management incentive plans.

Missing Wall Street analysts' consensus EPS estimates – even by just a penny – can result in significant downward pressure on stock prices. So, most management incentive plans included a very significant step at threshold, recognizing the sensitivity of this measure and providing a meaningful payout benefit for achieving the threshold EPS goal, which is often aligned with consensus EPS estimates. If a company missed consensus EPS estimates, there was a significant penalty in payouts for incentive plan participants: zero payout. The payout step served to align management incentives with shareholder outcomes.

With EPS as the performance measure, there was a rationale for a significant threshold payout step. However, this approach to payout curve design has been implemented far more widely than just for EPS-based incentives. It is now common to see a large threshold step payout for all financial measures and even many non-financial measures. It is also common for payout curves like those in

Figure 1 to be used not only for executives but also for other employee groups, like managers and professionals in sales, marketing, operations and functional support areas.

"Steps" in your incentive plan payout curve increase compensation risk unnecessarily. Smooth your curves and eliminate this risk.

The most common incentive plan payout designs provide a significant benefit for achieving a defined minimum level of performance. Viewed graphically, this "step" in the performance-payout relationship creates unnecessary business risks, and – more importantly – payout steps damage the pay for performance relationship. Small changes to incentive plan payout design can eliminate these risks and improve pay for performance.

"You get what you pay for" is accepted as a truism by compensation professionals. However, our experience has shown that compensation plans, in particular incentive plans, can at times lead to unintended results – results for which compensation committees may not wish to pay.

Compensation risk has existed ever since variable pay was introduced. Just as managers understood they could encourage behavior on targeted activities to improve performance results, employees quickly figured out how to adjust their behaviors and activities to maximize their own pay.

Poorly-designed incentive programs can even maximize employee pay while performance results are sub-optimal. At best, poorly designed incentives can result in counter-productive or dysfunctional behavior. At worst, these incentive programs can encourage poor customer outcomes and fraud.

We will discuss a slightly different compensation risk – one driven not by the measure of performance used (e.g. the number of new customer accounts opened), but rather increased risks that are a result of incentive plan design and the shape of the management incentive plan payout curve. Specifically, whether the incentive payout curve includes any "steps", and if so, the magnitude of such steps.

RISKS OF INCENTIVE PAYOUT STEPS

Most companies have realized that EPS is far less than an ideal measure of financial performance. As EPS has faded in popularity in favor of more meaningful measures of operating performance, the original rationale for incentive plan payout steps is gone.

More importantly, the steps in incentive plan payout curves may encourage inappropriate risk-taking and behaviors. Large steps have the potential to put management teams and Compensation Committees in a compromising position when performance results are expected to fall right around the threshold payout step.

Consider the situation in which year-end performance is expected to end up just short of the threshold payout step. How would management's behavior and decision-making change given the impact on individual incentive outcomes?

If performance results end up just above the threshold payout step, Compensation Committees and executives may wonder if short-term decisions were made simply to push performance over the payout threshold. Did mangers delay expenditures on training, development, hiring, equipment maintenance or even marketing? Did the sales and marketing team reduce prices or provide more favorable terms to customers to push volume and pull revenue forward from next year's first quarter into this year?

If decisions on these matters are influenced by individual incentive payments rather than solid operational and/or strategic reasons, then the incentive plan perversely introduces unnecessary business risks.

Potentially even worse is the situation in which performance results fall just short of the payout step.

Consider this potential discussion with the executive team or Compensation Committee: management could reasonably argue that some sort of payout is deserved, since they could have delayed expenditures or pulled revenue forward to this period to achieve the threshold goal, but avoided doing so because it risked longer-term sustainable performance.

Even without management's lobbying, the Compensation Committee might feel that the team deserves at least a small payout greater than zero, placing them in an awkward position relative to the original plan design and expectations, and potentially damaging the pay for performance relationship. Moreover, a non-zero payout sets a precedent that the Committee will provide some award, even for performance below threshold.

A BETTER ALTERNATIVE: ELIMINATE YOUR PAYOUT STEPS

So, how to address the risk associated with incentive plan payout steps? Consider one of two alternatives: (A) eliminate payout steps entirely, or (B) significantly reduce the "height" or magnitude of your payout steps.

ALTERNATIVE A. ELIMINATE PAYOUT STEPS ENTIRELY

Rather than setting a payout step for achieving the threshold performance goal (e.g., 50% of target at threshold), payout can begin at 0% at threshold. This approach eliminates potential gaming or inappropriate business decisions that may occur when performance is forecast to fall just short of the threshold as discussed above. An example of this approach is provided in Figure 2.

Figure 2. Remove Step for Threshold Performance

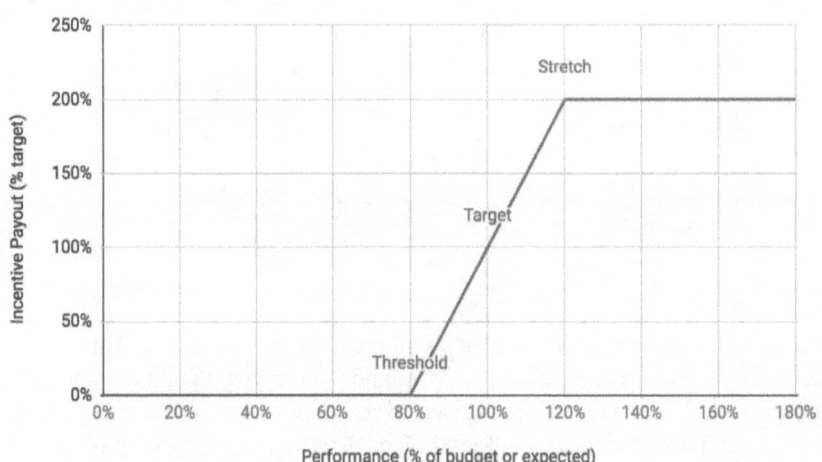

In this design, participants will earn a smaller payout at the same threshold level of performance (relative to the typical approach illustrated in Figure 1), but incremental improvements in performance are rewarded with a steeper payout curve. One way to ameliorate the impact of removing the threshold step is by easing the threshold performance goal. If, for example, the performance threshold was reduced to 60% a similar payment would be provided for 80% performance outcomes relative to the original stepped performance curve in Figure 1. See Figure 3 below.

Figure 3. Reduce Threshold Performance level

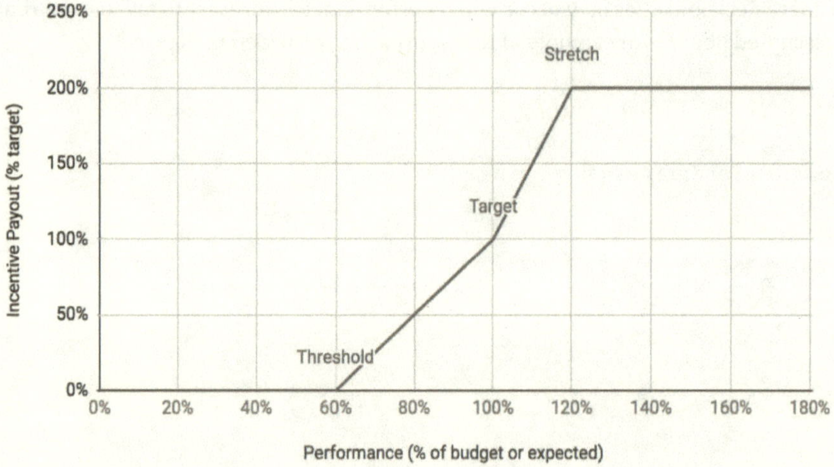

Note that in Figure 3 there is a steeper payout curve for above target performance. This indicates that incremental performance above target is valued more highly than incremental performance between threshold and target. An increase in the slope of the payout curve is often called an accelerator. Accelerators can have similar risks to steps, so consider your payout curve carefully and adjust as needed so incremental performance is appropriately rewarded between threshold, target and stretch goals.

ALTERNATIVE B. SIGNIFICANTLY REDUCE MAGNITUDE OF PAYOUT STEPS

If eliminating your payout steps seems too significant a change for your company to digest, then consider reducing the height of any steps. Instead of a payout of 50% of target for achieving threshold performance, reduce the threshold payout to 25% or 20%, see Figure 4.

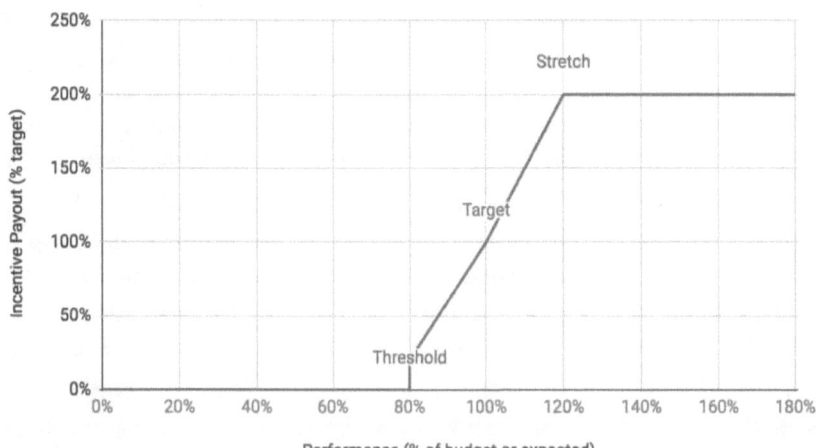

Figure 4. Reduce magnitude of payout steps

While the step and associated risk still exists, the magnitude is reduced through a smaller threshold incentive payment. Many companies have taken such an approach after concluding that a 0% payout would have been too much of a challenge to communicate to participants.

Another important risk mitigation strategy is to ensure that all final payments are subject to Compensation Committee discretion, rather that determined purely by a formula. Principles for discretion should be set in advance of any decision on payment outcomes, and can include things such as: material and unanticipated changes in the external environment (e.g., commodity pricing, forex, or regulation); changes in the internal business environment or strategy; or even adjustments for executive behaviors (e.g., risk-adjustments) and how results are achieved.

Long-term incentive steps add even more risk

All of these same risks apply to long-term incentive (LTI) programs with payout steps as well, and with potentially greater implications.

Many public companies have implemented (or are considering) LTI programs that measure total shareholder return relative to a peer group of companies (relative TSR, or rTSR). For example, a common design provides a threshold payout of 50% of target for achievement of rTSR at or above the 40th percentile of peers.

Consider the risks of the design described above.

As the company nears the end of the 36-month performance period, all participants should be able to estimate where their company's TSR falls relative to peers (and it is always a good practice for companies to regularly communicate this information to participants anyway). If rTSR is at the

39th percentile of peers, imagine the potential decisions the management team could make to push their company's rTSR over the threshold goal. Some of these decisions may not contribute to real, long-term, sustainable shareholder value, the intended outcome of an LTI plan.

Management may decide to communicate more aggressive internal expectations of performance for the following year; fast-track product releases or innovations; or communicate anticipated geographic growth, or discussions with potential M&A partners. Anything that increased rTSR an incremental point or two would have a significant effect on the earned compensation of the executive team.

Similar to the risk of diluting the pay for performance relationship described above, if rTSR falls just short of threshold, would the Compensation Committee feel compelled to make a discretionary award to participants?

Where LTI is a significant portion of total compensation, executives may come to undervalue this component of their reward if forecasts indicate that no payment will be made even if performance is only marginally short of the threshold. This devaluating of a whole portion of total compensation may also introduce retention or flight risk into the management cohort.

FINAL THOUGHTS

The design of incentive payout curves has not evolved significantly for quite some time. But with the additional focus on compensation risk, and the importance of aligning management to long-term sustainable shareholder value, now is the time to review incentive plans. Where there are risks associated with payout relationships that contain significant steps, Compensation Committees should eliminate those risks – or at least mitigate risk by reducing the height of those steps – by redrawing management incentive plan payout curves.

Compensation Committees should regularly review and adjust compensation plans to ensure plans continue to support the business strategy and effectively reinforce the pay for performance relationship. Eliminating or mitigating risk by addressing incentive payout steps can improve pay for performance alignment.

CHAPTER 7. FUNDING METHOD

HOW TO FUND?

For starts businesses need to decide on economic goals, amongst many are; return on investment, earnings per share, return on capital employed etc... Following, resonate on the formula for calculating the total bonus for a given year. As mentioned earlier, minimum threshold remains almost exclusively applied:

"the bonus pool will equal 10% of pretax profits after deducting 16% of invested capital as of the beginning of the year"

or alternatively, to exclude the investment valuation dilemma:

"3% of pretax earnings in excess of a 10% improvement over a weighted average of the past three years' earnings"

The company's strategy and hence its measures of performance will guide the source of funding. If corporate goals are the primary factor, the bonus pool would be directly related to corporate profits. If divisional performance is the driving factor, then divisional bonus pools should be utilized.

CHAPTER 8. CHANGE MANAGEMENT

When introducing any incentive compensation plan changes, consider these five steps to keep the sales team engaged and eager to meet their goals.

At a time of constant change and ever-growing competition, a company's sales compensation plan is one of the most powerful tools it has to improve sales performance by influencing sales behaviors. To be most effective, company leadership must ensure an agile approach to help the sales organization adapt to rapid changes in the market, competitive landscape and the company itself. But introducing any changes to how salespeople are compensated can be met with significant resistance, and if not handled properly, can lead to resentment, lower productivity, and higher turnover among the sales team at a time when they are needed most.

Still, incentive compensation plans are shown to have a strong and immediate impact on selling behaviors, making it crucial that any changes to the compensation plan must be well thought out and communicated from leadership down through the entire organization. How can this be accomplished? The following steps will set the right example and help the sales team not only prepare for change but embrace it and emerge successfully.

1. ANTICIPATE WHAT NEEDS TO CHANGE:

To remain competitive, organizations should seek to change their incentive compensation plans regularly. But it's important to do so in alignment with the dynamics of business reality. One of the biggest mistakes is assuming that any changes will remain in place throughout the year or even multiple years, without paying attention to what may change in the future. Instead, any changes or new processes should be designed through a series of "what-if" scenarios.

Some questions to ask include:

What kinds of plan rules lend themselves to frequent exceptions?

What kinds of exceptions are valid?

Are the processes being designed to handle exceptions?

Are there new plan rules that management considers tentative and likely to change?

Are there alternate plan rules or measures that might be considered if current plan rules or measures fail?

But it's not just about the changes to the compensation plans themselves; leaders must also anticipate changes in other processes and systems that can impact incentive compensation management. An example would be the introduction of a new HRIS system that may change how a transaction is credited to a sales person.

2. COMMUNICATE CHANGE ACROSS THE ORGANIZATION:

Although the need for change will often be clear, what's more challenging is actually implementing those changes. Key to success is having a clearly defined change management process, which entails thorough checklists, a master plan for making changes, published timelines for data processing and workflow procedures, and a well-defined escalation process for how various changes will be brought to the appropriate levels of management. Whether a change is a simple matter of re-crediting a transaction or involves more complex structural changes in data or systems, leadership must over-communicate and ensure everyone knows how the change will impact their daily roles.

3. ADDRESS THE KNOWN AND UNKNOWN ISSUES:

Every organization has a cycle for calculating and communicating incentive compensation results, whether on a daily, weekly, monthly, or quarterly basis. For this processing cycle to be most effective leaders must prepare their organizations for the known and unknown issues that care arise in order to minimize risks and any delays or errors. One common challenge stems from the need in many incentive plans to process data from prior periods along with the current period, leading to confusion over which transactions should be credited for which period. However, with clear business rules, proper planning, data validation, and results checking, such instances can be minimized.

4. PARAMETERIZE THE INCENTIVE COMPENSATION MANAGEMENT SYSTEM:

Being able to adapt to change easily should be a key requirement of any incentive compensation management system. This can be done by effectively using parameters to greatly reduce the time to make common changes and remove the need for hard coding. With good parameterization, it becomes faster and easier to make future plan changes, while resulting in improved accuracy and numerous other related benefits.

5. Look to automate key processes:

Many of the systems and processes used to manage incentive compensation grow organically and are touched by many hands over the years. This leaves a patchwork of manual, labor-intensive processes that increase the risk of delays and inaccuracies. The key to finding and fixing problems quickly is to step back and design an automated process. This will allow compensation analysts, who might otherwise spend a whole day sifting through reports to find errors and other issues, to shift from merely maintaining the system to being a proactive business partner who spends time on value add activities like performance analytics to help the sales organization proactively identify and adapt to unexpected changes.

A sales compensation plan should work to continually engage and motivate the sales team and keep them in alignment with company priorities. But any changes to how salespeople are compensated can have a serious impact on that delicate balance, resulting in increased administrative costs, lost revenue opportunities and resentment and increased turnover of your best sales talent. That is why the companies that can anticipate change and have a comprehensive strategy to address it from the top down will be best suited for success when they need to update their incentive compensation plans.

Conclusion

Designing an incentive rewards plan as discussed can vary considerably. Keeping in mind the company's administrative inheritance and top management's vision of how to influence corporate behavior. However, after understanding the alternatives and their implications an easier design selection is at hand. Exhibit 1 attempts to summarize the relationships among the aspects of incentive compensation plan and the three strategy problems considered in this analysis.

Exhibit 2 proposes an annual bonus plan that can be utilized by any company. Factors can be manipulated at each company's disposal according to requirements as discussed. It's not a one size fits all, but more of a smart adjustable solution aiding as an instrument of management control.

If you loved this book and want to get more information like this, subscribe to the newsletter for free at: https://www.bespokepublishinghouse.com/blog

EXHIBIT 1

Policy Issue	Financial Instruments	Performance Measures	Degree of Discretion	Size & Frequency	Funding Source
Product Life Cycle	Mix of cash bonus and stock options should reflect relevant timeline for top management	Qualitative and quantitative mix of measure according to relevant timeline	Formula based bonuses encourage focusing on the short run goals	Higher frequency bonuses encourage short term performance	
Market Dynamics	Bonus awards can enhance risk taking behavior	Qualitative measures assures executives of total performance evaluation	Formula based clarify rules therefore enhancing risk taking attitude	Bonus size must be adequate to the amount of risk involved and in line with the business	
Interdivisional Relationships		According to interdivisional cooperation, bonus pools can be based on divisional or corporate performance or ideally a mix of both	Formula based bonuses is best when little cross division efforts is required		According to the performance measures chosen
Corporate Relationships	Stock options directly link the interest of executives to corporate interest	Meaningful objectives measures of performance when top	Formula based bonuses are best with minimal corporate		Top management will have a stronger influence over

management only allocates resources, rather than actively running the business	interference managing the business. Discretionary bonuses otherwise	business units as long as the bonus pool is drafted from corporate profits. Ideally a mix of corporate and division profits should be used

EXHIBIT 2

ANNUAL BONUS PLAN PROPOSAL

BRIEF

This bonus plan aligns the bonus payment structure with overall business results of your Company, team results and performance appraisal ratings.

CONSIDERATIONS:

Market-competitive base-salary plan

Total cash compensation remains competitive

Ratio between base and variable/incentive pay

Proper appraisal and performance measurement tools

Value has to be assigned to various levels of contribution/result (how individuals affect team performance)

SALARY BANDS:

In establishing the award targets for the various levels of employees, the workforce is split into three groups, Non-management, Management and Executive. The higher the level an employee is in the company, the higher the percentage of pay the employee can earn via bonus. Each salary band ranges from current salary to Target Salary and Maximum Salary. It is recommended to base the Award on the Target Salary rather than the current salary. Please find below a proposal for this factor:

Salary Band	Award Target
1	10%
2	12%
3	17%

ON TARGET ACHIEVEMENT:

Next we need to determine what levels of financial results versus business targets or plans will trigger bonuses being paid or what percentage of the award targets will be paid. Below is a proposal for this factor:

Company Results versus Plan	Bonus Multiplier
Less than 90%	0%
90%-99%	50%
100%-110%	200%
111%-120%	240%
121% or more	300%

INDIVIDUAL PERFORMANCE INDICATOR:

Finally, we will need to determine a similar scale of multipliers based on Individual performance levels. These multipliers should be linked to performance appraisal ratings, providing a higher level of bonus to employees who meet and exceed performance objectives. Once again, a fixed multiplier can be used or a range can be established for flexibility to differentiate between employees who may be in the same Salary band and have the same performance rating, but where it is felt that some deserve slightly more reward than others.

Performance Rating	Individual Performance Multiplier		
	Min.	Default	Max.
Exceptional (E)	280%	300%	320%
Quality – High (QH)	230%	250%	270%
Quality – Solid (QS)	180%	200%	220%
Quality – Developing (QD)	50%	100%	150%
Improvement Required (I)	0%	0%	0%

REFERERENCES

1. See, for example, John Dearden, "The Case Against ROI Control," HBR May–June 1969, especially pp. 132–133.

2. Financial Motivation for Executives (New York, American Management Association, 1970), p. 244.

3. Mario Leo, "Executive Lures and Incentives in the Nation's Top 100," Business Management, March 1971, p. 29.

4. Towers, Perrin, Forster & Crosby, Inc., "Executive Bonus Awards and Stock Options in the Top 100 U.S. Industrial Companies," June 1971.

5. For a discussion of equitable pay, see my article, "What Is 'Fair Pay' for the Executive?" HBR May–June 1972, p. 6.

6. "Why Incentive Plans Fail," HBR May–June 1972, p. 58.

7. "Comp Targets That Work" Radhakrishnan Gopalan, John Horn, Todd Milbourn, HBRSep-October 2017

ABOUT THE AUTHOR

Ashraf Eltomi has held various leadership positions in Talent Management and Human Resources across six continents in the past fifteen years. Holds a BSc Industrial Engineering and an MBA with HR and Marketing focus.

He is a frequent contributor to publications on leadership and talent management, and has led international teams to multimillion profits.

Ashraf is currently Commercial Director at several international conglomerates. He co-developed BeSpoke Solutions Ltd, an International Organization offering Talent Management Services and Operational Efficiencies Solutions. In that role, his responsibilities included performance management, leadership development, and talent planning for over 5000 Associates. He also co-designed BeSpoke Publishing, a subsidiary of BeSpoke Solutions. His previous experience includes workforce analytics, compensation and HR generalist roles.

www.ingramcontent.com/pod-product-compliance
Lightning Source LLC
Chambersburg PA
CBHW030739180526
45157CB00008BA/3245